The Way of Biblical Justice

JOSÉ GALLARDO

HERALD PRESS
Scottdale, Pennsylvania
Kitchener, Ontario

THE WAY OF BIBLICAL JUSTICE
Copyright © 1983 by Mennonite Board of Missions,
    Elkhart, Ind. 46515
Published by Herald Press, Scottdale, Pa. 15683
    Released simultaneously in Canada by Herald Press,
    Kitchener, Ont. N2G 4M5
Library of Congress Catalog Card Number: 82-83386
International Standard Book Number: 0-8361-3321-8
Design: Alice B. Shetler/Art by Elmore Byler

83 84 85 86 87 10 9 8 7 6 5 4 3 2 1

Distributed overseas by Mennonite Board of Missions,
1251 Edom Road, Harrisonburg, Va. 22801

CONTENTS

PREFACE

Justice means different things to different people. Some persons define justice very narrowly. For them, it means the establishment of rights based on laws or rules. Others take a broader view of justice to mean well-being, righteousness, wholeness, peace.

Under the narrow understanding of justice, the wealthy and powerful are able to have the laws interpreted in their favor. In a strict sense, they are obeying the law, but taking advantage of the poor and the powerless.

The author, a biblical scholar and advocate for the poor, shows that biblical justice goes beyond law. It includes the concept of wholeness and well-being in all areas of life—social, religious, economic, and political. Grace and forgiveness are also important parts of the biblical understanding of justice.

The Way of Biblical Justice is volume 11 in the Mennonite Faith Series listed inside the back cover. It brings together important truths from both Old and New Testaments. The author also shows what this holistic focus meant for the Anabaptists of the sixteenth century and for us today.

Anyone wanting to pursue the theme further may check the references placed at the back of the book.

—J. Allen Brubaker

INTRODUCTION

Everyone looks for justice. Employees want their employers to be just. People want the government to be just. Someone who has been hurt wants justice to be done. The consumer wants just prices and measurements. We all want a more just society. Many struggle to establish this justice.

The normal human conscience is very sensitive to questions of justice or injustice. Nothing unites us more in a common cause than the call to safeguard basic human rights and freedoms. We all are moved to act on behalf of a person or group that is unjustly treated.

We see around us today injustice at all levels of

society. Therefore, a study of justice is urgently needed, as is the need for more just living.

Human Justice and Biblical Justice

Human justice is often thought of as the establishment of rights based on rules or laws. While laws should protect the weak and powerless, they often do not. Why? Because the wealthy and the powerful are able to have the laws interpreted in their favor. The biblical understanding of justice goes beyond law. It includes the concepts of well-being, wholeness, righteousness, and peace. This biblical concept of justice will help us to understand the difference between the Christian's conduct and that of society in general. In this booklet we will also study justice by comparing existing human models with Jesus' example of just living. This comparative study will inspire our conduct in favor of justice and help us set our standard of justice according to God's plan.

Our study begins with an overview of biblical justice. I then try to pull into focus a well-rounded view of biblical teaching concerning justice. For example, the history of the people of God reveals to us the just purposes of God. This Old Testament history also shows us the variety of meanings that encompass the biblical concept of justice. After looking at the law, the prophets, and the wisdom literature in the Old Testament, we will come to the revelation of God in Jesus. We will consider the teachings and example of Jesus and his apostles as our final authority on matters of justice. Even though the biblical revelation includes the law and the experiences of the Old Testament, Jesus is the fulfillment of

God's intent. What God did in Jesus is therefore equally valid for us today. He is the key for us to interpret the revelation of the Old Testament. By studying his life and teachings under the inspiration of the Holy Spirit in the community of disciples, we can interpret the Old Testament correctly.

The messianic era that Jesus came to inaugurate is still in operation. His teachings and life guide our conduct. The Holy Spirit continues to motivate us, the church, as it did in New Testament times. The Spirit enables us to live in agreement with the justice that God has established and to lead others to that same life. We will read the Bible and interpret it from the perspective of the cross of Christ. This viewpoint will cause us to see the fundamental difference between human justice and biblical justice.

1

LAW AND JUSTICE IN THE OLD TESTAMENT

PROBLEMS of injustice today are not really new. Only the people and situations are new. This truth hit me with new force several years ago when I was studying in Latin America. I was in missionary work in Bolivia, helping young people from Mennonite Central Committee. They were doing voluntary service for peace rather than serving in the United States military forces. They were helping the Bolivian people in a variety of ways: starting a home for orphans and children of the street, helping the highlands people find markets for their handcrafted goods, clearing virgin forests for native settlers, etc. An important task in colonization was cutting and burning the trees and underbrush of the forest. As the good land was cleared for cultivation, towns were formed, schools were built, and cooperatives were organized.

A Painful Contrast

The above effort to help the native people in a wholesome way contrasts with the unjust dealings of a large cotton company. The poor farmers of Santa Cruz were seriously abused. These farmers worked very hard to acquire their land and prepare it for cultivation. Then a large cotton company would come in and set up acquiring the land little by little. By dishonest actions, the company would put pressure on the owners of the small plots in order to acquire them. With the aid of large machinery to cultivate the land, the company added field to field until they got what they wanted. The company would not only pay very little for the land, but they would pay for it with alcohol. Why? So peasants would get drunk and consent to the sorry business with even less awareness.

Of course, the company owners and their agents reaped the benefits. The farmers, stripped of their land, soon became employees of the company. It paid them a miserable salary and provided terrible working conditions. For example, during the hot hours of the day water was not provided for them. Some lost too much body fluid and fainted from the heat. This is an example of some of the injustices denounced by the prophets:

> Woe to you who add house to house and join field to field till no space is left and you live alone in the land. Isaiah 5:8.

> Woe to those who plan iniquity, to those who plot evil on their beds! At morning's light they carry it out because it is in their power to do it. They covet fields and seize them, and houses, and take them. They defraud a man of his home, a fellowman of his inheritance. Micah 2:1, 2.

The Old Testament people of God—Israel—are rooted in Abraham, the father of the believers, the friend of God (Isaiah 41:8). Abraham walked in God's ways, doing justice and teaching his children to do the same (Genesis 18:19). Moses and the Exodus experience shed even greater light on right and wrong human conduct. The Ten Commandments and the laws that accompany them were designed to establish justice in Israel.

Moses and the Exodus

Moses had a great sense of justice. He could not stand the oppression of the weak. This caused him to use violence to defend the Hebrew from the ill treatment of an Egyptian. Because he killed the Egyptian, he had to suffer exile. As he cared for his father-in-law's sheep in the desert, he learned love and patience.

Later the people of Israel groaned because of their slavery in Egypt. They cried to God to take them out of bondage. God then chose Moses to act in his name and liberate his people from injustice. This process of liberation was slow and did not occur without suffering. But it is very clear that God hears the prayer of the oppressed, that God loves the poor and defends their cause. God frees the captives. God is a god of justice and a god of mercy. Because of this, "Moses answered the people, 'Do not be afraid. Stand firm and you will see the deliverance the Lord will bring you today.... The Lord will fight for you; you need only to be still' " (Exodus 14:13, 14).

Moses and the Judges

The first difficult experience in the desert caused the Israelites to murmur against Moses. It is easy to understand their anguish. They had walked three days without finding water. When at last they found some, it tasted so bad they could not drink it. God was testing the faith of his people through this experience. Moses turned to God in prayer. God heard his prayer and showed him how to purify the waters. There at Marah Moses gave the people some ordinances for the first time. He said, "If you listen carefully to the voice of the Lord your God and do what is right in his eyes, if you pay attention to his commands and keep all his decrees, I will not bring on you any of the diseases I brought on the Egyptians, for I am the Lord who heals you" (Exodus 15:26).

In this early period of Israel's history, Moses was responsible to exercise justice. He spent entire days seated, judging the people. Anyone that had a dispute came to him. He then judged between one and the other and declared God's ordinances and laws (Exodus 18:13-16).

However, when his father-in-law, Jethro, visited him, he saw that Moses was exhausted by the work. So he counseled him to spend more time before God. Jethro advised Moses to teach the people the decrees and laws and show them the way they should live. To lighten his load, Jethro counseled Moses to choose "men who fear God, trustworthy men who hate dishonest gain" and appoint them as authorities over the people. They would judge at all times and would bring only the difficult cases to Moses. "Moses listened to his father-in-law and did everything he said" (Exodus 18:21-24).

Sinai: The Tablets of the Law

The Ten Commandments given on Mount Sinai reveal the moral character of God and the requirements he has for his people. God wanted us to know that the quality of our relationships with others depends upon the quality of our relationship to God.

The first commandments concern God's sovereignty over his people. He is the liberator, the only one that deserves obedience. He is a just God and full of mercy; a jealous God, a God of power, a holy God. Everyone that honors God honors his father and his mother. Everyone that loves God, loves his neighbor, does not kill or rob or commit adultery; if we love God we do not lie or have wrong desires toward others or their goods.

Moses gives other orders to the people. Some of these are of a ritual character; others outline how to live together. Generally, they explain the Ten Commandments in more detail. These laws were given for the good of the people. They safeguard the rights of the poor, the slaves, the strangers, the women, and the land (see Exodus 21—23; Leviticus 19).

Above all, these laws have a preventative character. They were given to prevent wrong or avoid greater evil, to bring out the best in people. God's intention is that man, created for the best, participate in his holiness and reflect his image. The Law is then an instrument of salvation. It is a help, a

14

control for the changing and improvement of human conduct.

The Sabbatical Year and the Year of Jubilee

The laws Moses left the people of Israel concerning the land and the year of jubilee deserve special attention. The sabbatical year was a 12-month rest for the land (Leviticus 25:1-7). It is similar to the rhythm of work and rest that God observed in his creation. The land has rights, too. It shall not be exploited by making it produce year after year without rest. Thus, the sovereignty of God is affirmed and the fertility of the land is preserved.

Another important aspect of the sabbatical year was the remission of debts (Deuteronomy 15:1-11). Loans with no interest were to be given to any brother in need (Leviticus 25:36, 37). What had not been repaid by the seventh year was to be forgiven. God calls attention to a possible abuse during the sixth year. Some people would not want to lend during this sixth year for fear that the debtor would not repay. God considered it a grave sin by those who limited their generosity toward the poor in this way. Why? Because God protects the poor. God knows that the poor will always be with us. He, therefore, orders his people not to be stingy in lending to them. And if the poor cannot return what has been given them, the debt is to be forgiven in the sabbatical year. This practice was intended to safeguard the rights of the poor, to prevent a major separation of people into a rich and a poor class.

The sabbatical year favors the cause of the needy. It is a practical way to limit the abuses and injustices of the powerful. It is more a measure of justice than a measure of charity. The sabbatical, therefore, reflects sacred Law. It is not something that depends on the good will of the giver. We see here a practical way of sharing the holiness and justice of God.

By practicing the sabbatical, we become like God, rich in generosity and mercy. Helping the needy is a spiritual and material liberation for the one who gives and the one who receives. Forgiving debts also brings freedom and blessing to both giver and receiver. Therefore, when we give alms to a beggar and he responds, "God will pay you," let us not think him so mistaken (Proverbs 19:17).

The institution of the sabbatical year also provided for the liberation of slaves who had served for six years (Exodus 21:2; Deuteronomy 15:12-18). During those years of service he was to be treated not as a slave, but as any other worker (Leviticus 25:39, 40). This reminds us that, as the people of God, we are all his servants.

Under this Old Testament system, freedom was to be given to the servant who desired it in the sabbatical year or the year of jubilee (Leviticus 25:40). And he was not to be sent away with his hands empty: "Supply him liberally from your flock, your threshing floor and your winepress. Give to him as the Lord your God has blessed you" (Deuteronomy 15:14). By taking with him part of what he had produced by his work, he could remake his life.

The primary concern of the year of jubilee was to restore family property (Leviticus 25:8-17, 23-25). It occurred after every seventh sabbatical year or every forty-nine years. This year of recognition of God's plan led to a change in social relationships. All the properties, lands, and houses that were not within the walled city were returned to original families. Often these original owners had sold them to the rich because of their poverty at the time.

The year of jubilee was a unique year of grace: "Consecrate the fiftieth year and proclaim liberty throughout the land to all its inhabitants. It shall be a jubilee for you; each one of you is to return to his family property and each to his own clan. The fiftieth year shall be a jubilee for you; do not sow and do not reap what grows of itself or harvest the untended vines. For it is a jubilee and is to be holy for you" (Leviticus 25:10-12a).

In an agricultural society, land is the most important capital. To be deprived of land is to be without life. Therefore, God's order for the distribution and maintenance of property avoids unjust inequalities. The year of jubilee reestablished the socioeconomic order. This year of liberation is proclaimed because the earth and all life and property are God's. Men and women live free in a free land that yields fruit generously by the Lord of the heavens and the earth.

God is the Lord and owner. He is the liberator of his people, the restorer, the Savior. The sabbatical year and the year of jubilee demonstrate God's concern for socioeconomic structures. These celebrations revealed his plan to establish justice for his people. Although these practices were not always observed by the governors of Israel, the prophets remembered their importance (Ezekiel 45:8; 46:17). These leaders proclaimed the coming of a Messiah. In his day the liberation of the year of jubilee would finally be lived. Isaiah 61 announces this reality, which has its fulfillment in Jesus (Luke 4:21).

Living by the laws of the sabbatical year and the year of jubilee appear to be impossible in our society. But I believe it would be possible for Christians to live like this. Christians can form small groups with the purpose of pooling their economic assets for mutual aid. The richest communities would give loans without interest to the poorer communities. These would try to return the loans so others could enjoy the same benefits. In a similar way, capital would be invested in the form of aid; interest or profit would no longer be the most important goal.

2

THE MEANING OF JUSTICE IN THE OLD TESTAMENT

THE diamond stone receives its beauty from the harmonious reflection of all its sides. A flower is composed of different petals, some very similar to others. Each petal is needed to present the true image of the flower. A similar thing occurs in the biblical concept of justice. We cannot cling to a simplistic definition. We must look at several angles to obtain a more complete image.

Justice and Holiness

The Lord said to Moses, "Speak to the entire assembly of Israel and say to them: 'Be holy because I, the Lord your God, am holy.'"

Leviticus 19:1, 2.

> Do not pervert justice; do not show partiality to the poor or favoritism to the great, but judge your neighbor fairly. Leviticus 19:15.

Leviticus 19 shows us that justice is related to holiness. In this chapter we are told to share the holiness of God, to refrain from idol worship, and to help the poor and the stranger. Thus, faith in God prevents us from oppressing other persons. Leviticus 19 lists the laws regulating worship, social behavior, and magic. Notice that these laws which also prohibit adultery and occult practices are linked to just balances, just weights, and just measurements. Here we see that the Bible does not separate the personal and the social, the spiritual and the material. The one is closely connected to the other. God asks his people to be righteous in all their behavior, both toward God and toward others. When the Scribes asked Jesus which was the first commandment, he quoted Deuteronomy 6:4, 5: "The Lord our God, the Lord is one. Love the Lord your God with all your heart and with all your soul and with all your strength." Jesus tied this first great commandment to a second one: "Love your neighbor as yourself" (Leviticus 19:18). "There is no commandment greater than these," Jesus said (Mark 12:31). So justice is very closely related to how we relate to both God and our neighbors.

Justice and Welfare

We have just noted the biblical principle of unity between the material and the spiritual aspects of life. God also links together the exercise of justice and personal, familial, and social well-being. As a confession of faith the people of Israel affirmed:

> The Lord commanded us to obey all these decrees and to fear the Lord our God, so that we might always prosper and be kept alive, as is the case today. And if we are careful to obey all this law before the Lord our God, as he has commanded us, that will be our righteousness. Deuteronomy 6:24, 25.

Here justice and welfare are not only related, they have the same meaning. Living according to the will of God brings blessing and an abundance of riches (Deuteronomy 7:12-16; 28:1-14).

The Law doesn't link the promises of blessing only with obedience to the divine commandments. It also gives very serious warnings about a false trust in riches. For example, the people of Israel were not to forget that God chose them to be a special people, not because they were better than others. On the contrary, they were "the most insignificant of all the peoples" (Deuteronomy 7:7). The Lord chose them because of his love and made a covenant with them of love and mutual faithfulness.

God reminds us that there is an order of priorities. As Jesus taught, "A man's life does not consist in the abundance of his possessions" (Luke 12:15). For "man does not live on bread alone but on every word that comes from the mouth of the Lord" (Deuteronomy 8:3; Luke 4:4). The man of God who enjoys the wealth and the blessings that his faithfulness bring him maintains a humble and generous attitude. He lives a simple lifestyle, avoiding extravagance. His heart does not fall into pride, neither does he forget God. To the contrary, he shares his riches with the poor and recognizes that he needs to thank God for his well-being. Of course, God knows the hearts of men; he knows how easy it is for a man to take what is a gift and make it a right. Because of this, he gives a warning to Israel: "It is not because of your righteousness or your integrity that you are going in to take possession of their land ..." (see Deuteronomy 9:4-6).

Justice and Wisdom

Justice is closely related to knowledge and the right use of it. The book of Proverbs is a collection of wise sayings. The book was written to give wisdom "for acquiring a disciplined and prudent life, doing what is right and just and fair" (Proverbs 1:3). The term "justice" appears frequently in this book. However, it does not refer to the commonly understood legal attitude. Rather, Proverbs sees justice as a counterpart of wisdom. In other words, wisdom leads to justice. And wisdom and justice yield the fruit of spiritual righteousness. As Proverbs 2:7, 9 says, God "holds victory in store for the upright"; he who keeps his ear attentive to the voice of wisdom "will understand what is right and just and fair— every good path." Proverbs is very clear on this point: it deals not with human wisdom, but with wisdom that comes from God. "For the Lord gives wisdom, and from his mouth come knowledge and understanding" (Proverbs 2:6). The book also makes clear that God is on the side of the righteous. "For the Lord detests a perverse man but takes the upright into his confidence" (Proverbs 3:32).

The voice of wisdom speaks in the first person in Proverbs 8. Wisdom says she is "delighting in mankind" (v. 31) and promises to guide "in the way of righteousness, along the paths of justice" (v. 20). "For whoever finds me finds life" (v. 35). In a similar way, "righteousness delivers from death"

(Proverbs 10:2; 11:4). Why? Because "in the way of righteousness there is life" (Proverbs 12:28).

Proverbs contrasts the righteous person with the wicked and the foolish. The wise man is just because he fears the Lord and departs from evil. However, fools despise wisdom and discipline (Proverbs 1:7). The fool who wants to buy wisdom with money would make the wicked righteous and would condemn the just; it is a lack of understanding which God detests (Proverbs 17:15, 16).

Another aspect of wisdom is love for the poor. Frequently the Bible, especially Proverbs, contrasts the just and the poor to the fool or the wicked or the rich. These terms are used in many of the texts. The unjust who oppress the poor offend God, but he who has mercy on the poor honors God (Proverbs 14:31). God loves the poor so much that he who helps the poor is in effect lending to God. Proverbs 19:17 says God will reward him for the good he has done.

Justice and Salvation

Justice is closely related to salvation, too, as the following texts illustrate:

> For the Lord is righteous, he loves justice; upright men will see his face.
>
> Psalm 11:7.

Who may ascend the hill of the Lord?
Who may stand in his holy place?
He who has clean hands and a pure heart . . . he will receive blessing from the Lord and vindication from God his Savior. Psalm 24:3-5.
    The salvation of the righteous comes from the Lord; he is their stronghold in time of trouble. The Lord helps

23

them and delivers them; he delivers them from the
wicked and saves them, because they take refuge in him.
Psalm 37:39, 40.

The Psalms help us to know God's character and
his relationship with his people and his world. These
poetic writings inspire us to walk uprightly before
God. The believer who walks in the ways of the
Lord looks for justice and peace. The righteous man
is a man of peace (Psalm 37:37), and a man of faith
(Hebrews 11:4). In the hour of need God will save
him. The righteous puts his hope in the justice of
God and seeks his salvation (Psalm 119:123, 124,
174). He knows his hope is not in vain. He has the
confidence that God "will defend the afflicted
among the people and save the children of the
needy; he will crush the oppressor" (Psalm 72:4).

God does not want the innocent to suffer. The
strong abuse the weak and oppress them. But God
defends the cause of the weak. Being a righteous
judge, he saves those of a right heart and expresses
his wrath toward the wicked every day (Psalm 7:11).
God forbids his people from destroying the unjust.
Because "it is mine to avenge; I will repay," says the
Lord (Deuteronomy 32:35; Romans 12:19). For
"our God comes and will not be silent. . . . And the
heavens proclaim his righteousness, for God himself
is judge" (Psalm 50:3, 6).

The Messianic Justice

There is no guarantee of finding just judges in our
society. Power and fear make justice an instrument
of evil. The violence of the strong imposes its own
laws and the just lack justice when God is not the

judge. Because of this problem of injustice, God gives his people a messianic promise: the fulfillment of God's justice will be the salvation of his people. And in that salvation God will finally establish justice. The Messiah will exercise justice and bring salvation.

The psalmist announced this great event which the world hoped for. He saw the day in which "love and faithfulness meet together; righteousness and peace kiss each other. Faithfulness springs forth from the earth, and righteousness looks down from heaven.... Righteousness goes before him and prepares the way for his steps" (Psalm 85:10, 11, 13). Then all will recognize that "the Lord has made his salvation known and revealed his righteousness to the nations" (Psalm 98:2).

While writing these lines I was confronted with a case of injustice in democratic Spain. Two young men, Oscar and Jose, had come to our community looking for help. They wanted a change in their lives. They had just stolen a car and didn't know what to do. Our congregation counseled them to turn themselves in to the police. They agreed to do so. We promised to support them in everything.

The police were surprised when they turned themselves in. However, both the police and the judge were hard on them. The judge put them in jail. If we had not insisted on their right of freedom until convicted, they would have been left there until the day of their trial. Nobody knew when that might be. The police and the judge treated us badly also for being preoccupied with "those delinquents, plague of the society." However, they received the owner of the car very well since he had more money than we did. They also believed him and not us. They accepted as reasonable the amount he asked as compensation. According to many sources, that figure was five times more than normal. We could see that the judge was interested in defending the rich and condemning the poor. Justice had social interests. The owner of the car did not show interest in restoring the youth to responsible living. He was interested only in the money.

We sensed through this experience the suffering that the prophets of Israel felt at the oppression of the poor and the favoring of the rich. It should be noted that both the judge and the car owner claimed to be Christians. What should our attitude be toward injustice?

3

THE PROPHETS SPEAK ABOUT JUSTICE

THE prophets of the Old Testament had a conscience alert to the needs of the poor and oppressed. They denounced the corruption of the judges and rulers and announced the coming judgment of God. Isaiah exclaims: "Woe to those who make unjust laws, to those who issue oppressive decrees, to deprive the poor of their rights and rob my oppressed people of justice, making widows their prey and robbing the fatherless. What will you do on the day of reckoning . . . ?" (Isaiah 10:1-3).

For the prophets, injustice was not only a violation of the laws, but an offense to God's holiness. They considered fasting as blasphemy if there was no justice and mercy (Isaiah 58). God's response to the prayers of the people is on the condition that they "seek justice, encourage the oppressed. Defend the cause of the fatherless, plead the case of the widow" (Isaiah 1:15-17). Doing justice comes before any sacrifice, no matter how abundant (Micah 6:8).

Israel who had been called to be a light to the nations had become a rebellious people. Jerusalem, a city of justice and equality had become a place of murderers (Isaiah 1:21). Jeremiah laments that he cannot find anyone on the streets of Jerusalem who acts justly or looks for truth (Jeremiah 5:1). God had chosen these people as his vineyard. He did all he could for them, but they yielded bad fruit: "And he looked for justice, but saw bloodshed; for righteousness, but heard cries of distress" (Isaiah 5:7).

Against the Corruption of the Judges

Those who should have been guardians of justice were the first to be corrupt. The prophets were not afraid to attack the princes and governors of Israel. They denounced their abuses and called for repentance. The judges were sold to those in power. They received money as pay and deprived the poor of justice in the courts (Amos 5:12; Micah 7:3). They even justified the wicked (Isaiah 5:23).

Jeremiah could not stand the suffering of the poor and cried out to heaven for God to make justice. He was not silent before the king and his servants. In the name of God he demanded that the judges:

> Do what is just and right. Rescue from the hand of his oppressor the one who has been robbed. Do no wrong or violence to the alien, the fatherless or the widow, and do not shed innocent blood in this place. Jeremiah 22:3.

28

Ezekiel cries out against the oppression by the princes:

> You have gone far enough, O princes of Israel! Give up your violence and oppression and do what is just and right. Stop dispossessing my people, declares the Sovereign Lord. Ezekiel 45:9.

God has given authority to the judges and governors to maintain order and justice on the earth. But when these delegated authorities become corrupt, prophetic voices will be raised to denounce them. The authorities can punish us for such denouncements. However, the prophetic word has a spiritual power that goes farther than the eye can see. The truth has a power that overcomes evil. And although we may not see it, it should not impede our struggle for it. Sooner or later the victory will be seen.

From the Least to the Greatest

The prophets spoke not only against Israel's leaders, they also accused the people of having false and rebellious hearts. Each one sought his own gain: "They have become rich and powerful and have grown fat and sleek ... they do not defend the rights of the poor.... From the least to the greatest, all are greedy for gain" (Jeremiah 5:27, 28; 6:13).

The Israelites before the exile enjoyed great prosperity. They attributed this well-being to their privileged position with God and to the merits of their own righteousness. They believed their faith in one God made them superior to the pagan people around them. In summary, they were proud of knowing God and keeping his Law. But their religious ceremonies and outward expressions of faith were not accompanied by social justice. Instead, materialism had made them insensitive to the voice of God who spoke to them by the prophets. They did not object to increasing their riches at the cost of another's suffering. And in spite of this injustice, they boasted of knowing God. Because of this, Jeremiah warns them: "Woe to him who builds his palace by unrighteousness ... making his countrymen work for nothing, not paying them for their labor" (Jeremiah 22:13). The prophet reminds them that to know God they must defend the cause of the afflicted and the needy (Jeremiah 22:16). This kind of action brings divine blessing.

The prophet Amos called to repentance those who "cast righteousness to the ground" (Amos 5:7). He required the reestablishment of justice as a condition to receive pardon (Amos 5:15). The Lord detests people who commit injustices while singing songs of praise to him on beautiful instruments. He calls for justice to "roll on like a river, righteousness like a never-failing stream!" (Amos 5:21-24).

The Justice of God

God is holy. Nothing impure can dwell in his presence. God is just and he treats us with fairness. He is good beyond mere justice, for his acts are moved by mercy.

The prophets announced the fall of the people of Israel. The disobedience of the people finally brought their downfall. When considering the justice of God, we may tend to think only of punishment. But it is not the will of God that man should suffer. God loves his people and has provided

30

for them to live in truth, peace, and justice.

On the other hand, God has established spiritual laws which he cannot contradict. God will not prevent man from doing evil, if that is man's choice. Man incurs his own destruction by his disobedience. God warns, announces, persuades, does everything he can to remove man from evil. However, man is free to rebel against God. God hurts deeply because of those who depart from his ways. He does not rest until his voice is heard. He wants to bring all men to himself. But even the people of God suffer the wages of sin. Because God is just, he is partial to no one. "The soul who sins is the one who will die" (Ezekiel 18:4). However, the Lord does not want us to die the death of sin. He wants us to "repent and live" (Ezekiel 18:32).

The nation of Israel was destroyed as the prophets had announced and captives were taken to Babylon. This was the outcome of their pride and unfaithfulness. The test of the exile caused them to recognize their transgression and to ask God to forgive them. Daniel confesses, "We have sinned and done wrong. We have been wicked and have rebelled; we have turned away from your commands and laws. We have not listened to your servants the prophets, who spoke in your name to our kings, our princes and our fathers, and to all the people of the land. Lord, you are righteous, but this day we are covered with shame ..." (Daniel 9:5-7). Daniel recognizes that the tribulation God brought to the people of Israel is an expression of his justice: "For the Lord our God is righteous in everything he does; yet we have not obeyed him" (Daniel 9:14). The justice of God cannot overlook disobedience to divine principles.

But the emphasis in justice need not be punishment. The biblical concept of divine justice focuses on helping the righteous, defending their cause, and liberating the oppressed. The justice of God is manifested as much in his love for righteousness as in his hatred toward sin; in his blessings on the faithful righteous as in the disgraces that accompany the acts of injustice. The justice of God is seen above all in the protection and victory that he gives his faithful people over all their adversaries (Psalm 98:1-3). The justice of God is manifested in his faithfulness to fulfill his promises (Nehemiah 9:7, 8). The justice of God is manifested in this: his promises are always promises of justice, and justice always brings salvation. As the Lord says by the prophet Isaiah: "Listen to me, my people; hear me, my nation: The law will go out from me; my justice will become a light to the nations. My righteousness draws near speedily, my salvation is on the way, and my arm will bring justice to the nations" (Isaiah 51:4, 5).

God promised Israel that he would reestablish justice among his people and in all the earth. A righteous Messiah, a faithful king, a servant of God, upright and obedient would bring it to pass. Jeremiah announces it like this:

> "The days are coming," declares the Lord, "when I will raise up to David a righteous Branch, a King who will reign wisely and do what is just and right in the land. In his days Judah will be saved and Israel will live in safety. This is the name by which he will be called: The Lord Our Righteousness. Jeremiah 23:5, 6.

The prophets identified the just and the poor. They were the ones sold into slavery because they could not pay their debts (Amos 2:6). The prophets had also shown God's favor toward the poor and humble in spirit (Isaiah 11:4; 66:2). It is not strange then that the coming Messiah is described as a humble servant who will bring justice to the nations. The chosen one of God "will not shout or cry out.... A bruised reed he will not break, and a smoldering wick he will not snuff out. In faithfulness he will bring forth justice" (Isaiah 42:1-4).

Not only will the Messiah be poor, but he will be a servant before God. And not only a servant, but a suffering servant. Though innocent, he would be punished for the wickedness of the powers of this world. "He had no beauty or majesty to attract us to him, nothing in his appearance that we should desire him. He was despised and rejected by men, a man of sorrows, and familiar with suffering. Like one from whom men hide their faces he was despised, and we esteemed him not" (Isaiah 53:1-5). By this poor innocent one God brings us his justice, his salvation.

This righteous, humble, poor Messiah will know what the justice of God is because he will be that justice. His life will be one of upright obedience to God, but God in his mercy will permit the punishment to fall on him that would fall on the unjust. God will be just with him in that he will not leave sin unpunished. Knowing that the wages of sin is death, the suffering servant will die for the sins of the world. His innocence and faithfulness will give God the right to maintain eternal justice. Through the suffering servant, God will show men the way of justice among them and the way of justification before him.

In announcing his coming, Isaiah saw the surprising justice of this suffering servant: "He will not judge by what he sees with his eyes, or decide by what he hears with his ears; but with righteousness he will judge the needy, with justice he will give decisions for the poor of the earth. . . ." His weapons will not have the violence of the world's weapons. His word will be his powerful weapon: "He will strike the earth with the rod of his mouth; with the breath of his lips he will slay the wicked. Righteousness will be his belt and faithfulness the sash around his waist" (Isaiah 11:3-5). The suffering servant, the promised Messiah will not combat his enemies with might nor with power, but by the Spirit of God (Zechariah 4:6).

4

JESUS AND JUSTICE

MARY, inspired by the Holy Spirit, prophesied concerning the Messiah. One of his attributes would be the righteous judge. Mary affirms the hope of the prophets of Israel: God "has scattered those who are proud in their inmost thoughts. He has brought down rulers from their thrones but has lifted up the humble. He has filled the hungry with good things but has sent the rich away empty" (Luke 1:51-53). Mary here describes the justice of God that would take place in the messianic era. These are truly revolutionary ideas. It is a program that only God with his mighty arm could bring to pass. He will create a kingdom of servants who at last live in accordance with his truth and his justice.

When John the Baptist started preaching about the coming of the Messiah, calling people to repentance, many came to him. In light of the coming messianic judgment, the people asked, what shall we do? He answered: "The man with two tunics should share with him who has none, and the one who has food should do the same." To the tax collectors he said, "Don't extort money and don't accuse people falsely—be content with your pay" (Luke 3:8-14). These were fruits worthy of repentance, fruits of justice, fruits of salvation. Mary and John were not speaking of a purely spiritual religious experience. Rather, all of life and conduct entered into the spiritual change that the Messiah brought.

The prophets and biblical writers made no separation between the spiritual and the material, worship and everyday life, religious experience and conduct in general. They saw all aspects of life as one whole. In our understanding of faith and Christian practice, we, too, often separate them. This can easily lead to empty religion and injustice.

The Liberating Messiah

On one occasion when Jesus went to the synagogue on the Sabbath as was his custom, he stood to read. He was given the book of the prophet Isaiah and he read:

> The Spirit of the Lord is on me, because he has anointed me to preach good news to the poor. He has sent me to proclaim freedom for the prisoners and recovery of sight for the blind, to release the oppressed, to proclaim the year of the Lord's favor.
>
> Luke 4:18, 19; Isaiah 61:1, 2.

And Jesus added, "Today this scripture is fulfilled in your hearing." They were all amazed and asked, "Isn't this Joseph's son?" Why were the people surprised about what Jesus had said? Not only because he applied to himself the prophecy of Isaiah and the program of the Messiah. They also were surprised because the prophecy declared that the Messiah would bring peace, freedom, and justice—justice as enjoyed in the sabbatical year and the year of jubilee. However, Jesus would bring a greater degree of justice, and it would have an eternal meaning.

When John the Baptist heard about Jesus' work, he sent his disciples to ask him if he was the Messiah. Jesus did not answer yes or no. He merely said, "Go back and report to John what you have seen and heard: The blind receive sight, the lame walk, those who have leprosy are cured, the deaf hear, the dead are raised, and the good news is preached to the poor" (Luke 7:22). Jesus' answer not only reported what he was doing. It also quotes almost literally the prophecies of Isaiah on the messianic hope of liberation (Isaiah 35:5, 6; Isaiah 61:1, 2).

This liberation that the prophets announced, and which Jesus fulfilled affects every area of our lives. It involves the whole person—body, soul, and spirit. It touches all the dimensions of social, religious, economic, and political life. The year of jubilee was not only a time of rest for the earth, of forgiveness of debts, restitution of family property and liberation of slaves. It was also a time to be reconciled with enemies, to make atonement of sins, to receive inner healing (Leviticus 25:9). When Jesus announces that he brings the messianic era, he calls the poor—

the outcasts of Israel—the faithful remnant. He makes a new covenant with them sealed by his blood. His daily obedience to the Father not only leads him to live for others, but also to give his life so they can live.

The Justice of the Kingdom

Jesus called twelve disciples and gave them a program of action. He explained and demonstrated the conduct expected of participants in his plan of salvation, of citizens in his kingdom.

Chapters 5 to 7 of the Gospel of Matthew give the disciples specific teachings on messianic justice. This justice was much greater than the justice of the scribes and Pharisees (Matthew 5:20). Jesus goes further than simply fulfilling the law. He presents the original intention of God for man. This justice calls happy and blessed the poor in spirit, those who mourn, the meek, those who hunger and thirst for righteousness, the merciful, the pure in heart, and the peacemakers. Those who hunger and thirst for righteousness will not only be blessed, but also filled. And the kingdom of heaven belongs to those who suffer persecution because of righteousness. As the prophets were persecuted for righteousness, so Jesus was persecuted. By living this way, Jesus' disciples would be following in his steps, participating in his messianic task (Matthew 5:1-12).

The justice of the kingdom implies a radical conduct that is possible only in Jesus. Now, not only is killing unjust, but even an insult is considered a form of homicide. Adultery is not only prohibited, but every lustful glance is considered adultery. Divorce is not permissible for a disciple of Jesus.

Swearing is unnecessary, because he who loves God never lies. The justice of the kingdom condemns violence in all its forms. Jesus calls us to resist evil and love our enemies.

Jesus teaches his disciples to have a relationship of justice, not only with men, but also with God. This justice is not to be a mask before men that gives the appearance of kindness. Jesus condemns this appearance of righteousness in the Pharisees. He calls his followers to live in the truth without show. Fasting, giving alms, prayer, all have a new meaning to the disciple of the kingdom. The justice of the kingdom is much more important than any other interest. Jesus calls those who follow him to seek first the values of the kingdom and things will take second place. Those needs will be provided for as a result of the justice of God, of the order of his kingdom (Matthew 6:25-34).

The justice of the kingdom will be the standard the Messiah will use when he judges the world at the end of time. In this judgement of the nations, the King will call the inheritors of the kingdom blessed. They gave the hungry something to eat, gave drink to the thirsty, invited the stranger in, clothed the naked, visited the sick, and went to see those in prison (see Matthew 25:31-46). These will be the ones to reign eternally with him according to the justice of God. They will be the righteous of the Lord, for they counted the price of obedience and lived according to the will of God. At the end of time "The angels will come and separate the wicked from the righteous" (Matthew 13:49). "Then the righteous will shine like the sun in the kingdom of their Father" (Matthew 13:43).

Jesus and the Pharisees

Jesus' greatest conflicts were with those who had a false concept of justice. He strongly confronted the scribes and Pharisees. They knew the law and vigorously enforced all the ceremonial laws, such as washing the hands and keeping the Sabbath. This achievement led them to hold a high opinion of themselves and to scorn others. They were proud because they trusted in their own righteousness.

The Pharisees believed themselves superior to others because of what they could do in their own strength. They forgot that God wanted to save mankind with those laws that they observed so strictly. On one occasion the scribes and Pharisees were spying on Jesus to see if he would heal on the Sabbath. The Sabbath had been set aside by God as a day of restoration, of rest, of peace and well-being. All of this was for man's welfare and to bring him closer to God. That is why Jesus asks them: "Which is lawful on the Sabbath: to do good or to do evil, to save life or to destroy it?" (Luke 6:9). Jesus heals on the Sabbath to fulfill the justice of God. This act offends the righteousness of the scribes and Pharisees. They seek to destroy him, because they feel he is going against the law to heal on the Sabbath (Mark 3:6).

Jesus spoke forcefully to those who "were confident of their own righteousness and looked down on everybody else" (Luke 18:9). He said, "There is more rejoicing in heaven over one sinner who repents than over ninety-nine righteous persons who do not need to repent" (Luke 15:7). Jesus noted that in the kingdom of heaven "everyone who exalts himself will be humbled, and he who humbles himself will be exalted" (Luke 18:14).

Jesus and Power

It is difficult for the rich to enter the kingdom of God (Luke 18:24). The rich are self-sufficient and in their abundance don't need God, but the kingdom of God belongs to the poor (Luke 6:20). Jesus, therefore, teaches his disciples not to seek greatness in the eyes of men: "Beware of the teachers of the law. They like to walk around in flowing robes and love to be greeted in the marketplaces and have the most important seats in the synagogues and the places of honor at banquets" (Luke 20:46). Jesus also told his disciples not to seek power like the rulers of the nations who lord it over them and call themselves benefactors. "Instead, whoever wants to become great among you must be your servant, and whoever wants to be first must be your slave—just as the Son of Man did not come to be served, but to serve, and to give his life as a ransom for many" (Matthew 20:26-28).

Jesus and Religiosity

In Matthew 23 Jesus launched an attack against the justice of the scribes and Pharisees. He exposed the contradictions between their love of the law and their false justice. Jesus calls them hypocrites, or play actors. They were not true men because with their show of religion they obstruct the work of God. Under the pretext of obeying the law, they do the opposite of what God wants. They are obsessed with achieving merit by fulfilling the details of the law. They tithe mint and cummin and leave out the most important part of the law: justice, mercy, and faithfulness (Matthew 23:23).

Jesus does not want to take away their correctness

41

in the small things. Rather, he asks that they not neglect doing the basic truths of God's Word. What Jesus condemns is this: on the outside they appear righteous, but on the inside they are full of iniquity. They are like whitewashed tombs, clean on the outside but unclean inside (Matthew 23:27, 28).

That is why Jesus prefers to eat at the house of a sinner like Zacchaeus. Jesus knows that the sinner can repent and receive the salvation that he preached. Zacchaeus, who was a very rich man, gave half of his riches to the poor and returned four times the amount to those he had cheated (Luke 19:1-10). But the religious leaders were too proud to repent. They refused to admit their sin.

Because of their hard hearts, the scribes and Pharisees could not comprehend the justice Jesus required of them. So they asked themselves why He ate with the publicans and sinners. Jesus told them: "Go and learn what this means: 'I desire mercy, not sacrifice.' For I have not come to call the righteous, but sinners" (Matthew 9:13).

Today in our churches we find the same dilemmas and conflicts that Jesus found. Therefore, we must remain faithful to the life and teachings of Jesus. We must avoid acting like the Pharisees—using laws to justify evil (Mark 7:9-13). Using religion to control people is a very subtle temptation. Siding with the poor and those who suffer will free us from falling into the false justice of the powerful. They use money and wealth to retain their privileges, often by finding "holes" in the laws of the land.

Justice and Mercy
Those who want to see in Jesus a purely legal con-

cept of justice will be very perplexed. For Jesus, justice is not a matter of simply rewarding the good and punishing the evil. The Old Testament shows us the close relationship between the justice of God and the salvation that the world hopes for and needs. The prophecies concerning the Messiah emphasize this connection between the justice and salvation of God. Certainly God is just and the wicked bring on themselves the consequences of their wickedness. But God is more interested in forgiveness than in punishment. He gives the abundance of his love to reach all men if they will only repent. For even though God is just, his mercy is also very great.

The parables and the life of Jesus show us God's character. God is shown as a loving father. For example, he continually waits for the return of the son who left him in rebellion and wasted his money on vices. When the son returns, the father pours out his love and generosity to celebrate his coming (Luke 15:11-32). Or God is presented as a king. Although he is demanding and just, he is moved to mercy by the pleas of a servant and forgives his debt. This king also requires justice. When the forgiven servant is not merciful with his fellow servant who owes him much less, the king is very angry. He throws the unjust servant into jail again until he pays the whole amount he owed. God expects us to forgive others, just as we have been forgiven. God expects us to forgive our brother who sins against us as many times as he sincerely repents of his sin (Matthew 18:21-35; Luke 17:3, 4). This is why mercy and forgiveness are part of the justice of the kingdom of God. This is why we cannot expect to be forgiven by God if we are not willing to forgive him who owes us something or has offended us (Matthew 6:12-15). Because God is merciful and just, we are called to share mercy and live in the justice of salvation.

God's righteous acts may sometimes perplex us. He retains the right to break molds and the so-called rights of men. An example is the good landowner who hired the unemployed in his vineyard. When he contracted the workers, he promised to give them a just wage. He agreed to give the first ones a denarius for the day, and they accepted it as just. But they were surprised and angry at the end of the day when they saw that the last ones who had come to work received the same. Those who had worked less actually received more per hour. Out of concern for human justice, the first workers protested. We might say, they had reason to protest. But the landowner does not change his mind. Conscious of justice, he says to one who protests: "Friend, I am not being unfair to you. Didn't you agree to work for a denarius? Take your pay and go. I want to give the man who was hired last the same as I gave you. Don't I have the right to do what I want with my own money? Or are you envious because I am generous? So the last will be first, and the first will be last" (see Matthew 20:1-16). The landowner was being just. He paid the fair wage each had agreed upon.

The Death of the Righteous One

Jesus died as did all the prophets. And Jerusalem reserved the same treatment for him: a violent death (Matthew 23:34-37). It was not something that surprised him. Although it was very hard to accept, Jesus obeyed the Father to this bitter end. He often announced his death to his disciples, although they did not comprehend his meaning (Matthew 16:21-23). When he believed that the time had come, Jesus "resolutely set out for Jerusalem" (Luke 9:51). He well knew what awaited him there. He would be handed over, tried, and condemned to death. He had prepared himself for this step, and he had also prepared his disciples (Matthew 10:21-24; 24:9). His death was not merely the fulfillment of prophecies, but the logical outcome of his radical obedience to the Father. His death cannot be separated from his life. He suffered and died to establish the justice of the kingdom. This is the only way his life could end. Although tragic, his crucifixion was the most normal conclusion. He confronted the political-religious powers of his time, and so he had to die (Luke 17:25 and Matthew 26:66).

At Jesus' trial it was evident that a righteous one was being condemned. Pilate's wife shared with her husband her conviction that Jesus was righteous (Matthew 27:19). This same Pilate declared to the Jewish people before handing Jesus over to be crucified: "I am innocent of this man's blood" (Matthew 27:24). Even the centurion, after seeing Jesus' conduct during his passion and death, gave glory to God. He exclaimed when he saw him die: "Surely this was a righteous man" (Luke 23:47). The apostle Peter in his sermon after Pentecost reminded the Jewish people that they had disowned "the Holy and Righteous One" (Acts 3:14). Shortly before Stephen was stoned to death for following Jesus, he rebuked his opponents for being like their fathers:

"Was there ever a prophet your fathers did not persecute? They even killed those who predicted the coming of the Righteous One. And now you have betrayed and murdered him" (Acts 7:52).

Jesus, Our Righteousness

The center of Christian faith is found in the meaning of Christ's death. It is most important to understand and experience the meaning of Jesus' death on the cross. We will focus now on the ethical implications of his death rather than the doctrinal or spiritual meaning. The cross leads us to live more fully the scope of the salvation that God offers humankind.

We have already seen that God is a just God. Not only is he good, he is also judge. We know that the unavoidable end of sin is death (Romans 6:23).

But God loves the sinner. Morally speaking, how can God take our sin seriously and at the same time offer us salvation? Jesus' death solves the problem. God's Word reveals this truth.

God, in Jesus, took upon himself the consequences of sin—death. "Very rarely will anyone die for a righteous man, though for a good man someone might possibly dare to die. But God demonstrates his own love for us in this: While we were still sinners, Christ died for us" (Romans 5:7, 8). After having declared that man should die, the righteous judge carries out his justice. But to save the condemned, the judge dies in his place. The violence that should have been justly unleashed against us, God took upon himself in Jesus.

Obedience to God's will and purpose caused Jesus to suffer the consequences of sin at the hands of sinners. Everyone who puts his faith in Jesus pleases the Father as Jesus pleased him. The sinner is, thereby, transformed into Jesus' image by the spiritual power that comes through his death on the cross. By his death, Jesus took upon himself the condemnation of the sin of the world. In spite of the injustice of men, God does not make them pay the price of their sin. Rather, in his love he suffers that injustice so that man can be saved. Thus, God rescues the man condemned to die. God atones for his guilt by letting Jesus die in his place. Thus is manifested the justice of God who, in Jesus, is both judge and the one who justifies. Now God declares righteous everyone who recognizes the mercy of God, repents from his sins, and identifies with the death of Jesus, the Righteous One. The believer who recognizes the inadequacy of his own righteousness can now receive the power of God. This is the same power that resurrected Jesus from the dead to live a new life. And this is a free gift of God! Being just, he takes upon himself in Jesus the consequences of his justice. He, thereby, shows his love by forgiving the guilt of our rebellion. By Jesus' death, believers are freed of the weight of sin and equipped to live a life of salvation. . . . "Do not offer the parts of your body to sin, as instruments of wickedness, but rather offer yourselves to God, as those who have been brought from death to life; and offer the parts of your body to him as instruments of righteousness" (Romans 6:13).

We have noted that God is just and that he exercises justice. However, his way of doing justice is not common among men. His justice grows out of his love for us. Both his love and justice go together.

His plan to overcome the vicious circle of injustice is to take upon himself the violence that it produces. This releases us and gives us the opportunity to renew our lives in Jesus. We then can learn to live, not only for ourselves but also for God. In Christ, we are conformed to the justice of God of which he is not only a receptor but also a bearer. God's kind of justice is also the best way for us to exercise justice. God did not come to us as a violent warrior or a judge without love. In Jesus, God came humbly, submitted, obedient, quiet. His power was in his words and in his love lived even unto death (John 13:1). Jesus, the Righteous One, is declared the judge. But he is a meek, broken judge. He takes upon himself the violence of evil rather than imposing it on others. And by dying on the cross he shows us how to respond to violence and work for justice. Jesus is not only the righteousness of God for our salvation; he is also our way of exercising justice in the world, of working for the salvation of those who will believe in him.

The Strategy of the Cross

Whoever claims to live in him must walk as Jesus did. 1 John 2:6.

If you know that he is righteous, you know that everyone who does what is right has been born of him. 1 John 2:29.

This is how we know what love is: Jesus Christ laid down his life for us. And we ought to lay down our lives for our brothers. 1 John 3:16.

A Style of Life

Jesus did not see his ministry as finished after the

resurrection. In reality, that was the beginning of his messianic ministry for all humanity. His ministry continues through his disciples who are empowered by the Holy Spirit. Jesus had promised to send the Spirit as a comforter, guide, and moving force. He then commissioned them to carry out his work. Jesus said, "Peace be with you! As the Father has sent me, I am sending you" (John 20:21).

Jesus continued his messianic task through the disciples who had believed in him. He drew them to himself and transformed them. He also sent them with total authority to present the plan of salvation: announce the forgiveness of God, and be living witnesses of the transforming power of the cross. They would proclaim the victory of life over death. They would also be life and enliven others by the power of the Word and of life. Jesus would be with them every day until the end of the world (Matthew 28:20). The disciples were asked to live the light of the life of Jesus, participating in his plan of salvation for humanity. The cross is our model of conduct, our style of life.

Love and Nonviolence

We are called to live and suffer for justice as Jesus did. The plan of the cross is the strategy of love and nonviolence. In our struggle for social justice among men we cannot lose sight of the example that God has given us. Confronted by conflict, we are called to act so that truth and justice will be done. But our goal is salvation of the unjust, not their destruction. In Christ we detest injustice and believe in the possibility of change. When confronted with the rebellion of the wicked, we will never employ violence to destroy them. Rather, we will, with God's help, pay the price of suffering as Jesus did. We will be willing to suffer and lose our lives for the cause of justice. Jesus teaches us that sacrifice is a fountain of blessing (Matthew 5:10). It has in it the spiritual power to transform evil to good (Romans 12:21). All of this is weakness and foolishness in the eyes of men. However, it is the power of God and wisdom of God for those who understand the way of the cross (1 Corinthians 1:23, 24). If our end, like God's, is the liberation of man in every aspect of his being, we must use means consistent with that end.

Our Weapons of Combat

We dare not contradict Jesus' nonviolent example to obtain justice in conflict situations. Even though our peaceful response seems to have failed, we may never resort to violence. In spite of hardship, our commitment will be that light and truth reign. The world believes justice is done when the guilty are punished or when they have made amends for the wrongs they have done. In extreme cases it is believed necessary to destroy the life or the possessions of the unjust. Our worldly systems of justice often pursue such ends even though the unjust does not recognize his guilt. However, Christians know that in the end their "struggle is not against flesh and blood [persons, matter], but against the rulers, against the authorities, against the powers of this dark world and against the spiritual forces of evil in the heavenly realms" (Ephesians 6:12). "For though we live in the world [in our mortal body], we do not wage war as the world does [according to the strategies of the man of sin]. The weapons we fight with are not the weapons of the world. On the contrary, they have divine power to demolish strongholds." (2 Corinthians 10:3, 4).

A Revolutionary Strategy

Having understood God's purpose in the cross, Paul confronts a problem of relationships in the Christian community of Philippi. He asked them to act with humility and meekness, like Jesus. He made himself obedient, even to death on the cross, to reconcile men to God and reconcile men to each other (Philippians 2:5-11). In the same way, the apostle Peter calls Christians to be willing to suffer unjustly. Peter notes that Jesus suffered for us, leaving for us an example that we should follow in his steps. "When they hurled their insults at him, he did not retaliate; when he suffered, he made no threats. Instead, he entrusted himself to him who judges justly" (see 1 Peter 2:19-23).

When we live in obedience to Christ, we do not let efficiency or profit govern our actions. The true revolution in society is not based on violence, for it would need to be maintained by the use of arms. Rather, the true revolutionary approach looks for a more just society where God's peace reigns. This approach uses means that correspond to the end. Therefore, God has provided the way of the cross to create a society of forgiveness and reconciliation. Here justice and mercy freely reign. No force or violence is needed.

5

WE FACE ISSUES OF JUSTICE

THE community in which I live was once going through hard times economically. We had rented a house in town to help youth who were involved with drug abuse and crime. Meanwhile, we were remodeling a large house we had purchased. The rent for the house in town was 5,000 pesetas above the normal rate. It, therefore, seemed excessively expensive. We felt the rent was unjustly high. Every month we owed them 15,000 pesetas. The idea arose of asking the owners to lower the rent. Although it was too much for us, we needed that house. It was the only one in town we could rent while we remodeled ours. But when housing is scarce, rent is more likely to be raised than lowered.

The more we thought about asking for a reduction in rent, the more foolish the idea seemed. The owner was a difficult character. Her main concerns were materialistic. If she had had the courage, she would have asked for even higher rent in the beginning. She would, no doubt, wonder why we were coming to discuss lower rent now. After all, we had made an agreement and paid several months. But we all felt the owner had been unjust with us. That house should not have rented for more than 10,000 pesetas. This would have been just, possibly even on the high side still.

We prayed about it and decided to act. Armed with courage we entered the battle. We sensed a need to challenge logical reasoning and act for justice. We took a step of faith and obtained what we asked for. To my great surprise, the lady agreed to lower the rent to 10,000 pesetas. It was not without difficulty. However, I still don't know what changed her mind. It does not matter. The incident shows how even a Christian community can fall into the same negative thinking of those who do not know the God of power.

God's Standards

The decisions of modern man are clouded by doubt about the future of society. People, therefore, look for fast and efficient results. And because the time is short and the future uncertain, people worry. The pain and suffering of the present argues against a more time-consuming course of action. It is even considered important to reach the proposed end regardless of the actions involved.

These low moral standards are even accepted by comfortable Christians. Some well-organized groups that strive for justice and social change also follow low standards. The efficient is that which works the fastest, which touches the most people.

These criteria of efficient planning and production, however, have severe limits for entering God's kingdom. As Isaiah 55:8 says, our thoughts are not his thoughts nor our ways his ways. In God's realm, the quality of the result and how it is achieved is more important than quantity and efficiency. He is very much interested in the means we use to reach the end result, however just and good it may be. God teaches us to walk in his ways. Though they may appear strange and a bit unreasonable, they are certainly wiser and of better quality. God invites us to trust in him even though at first it seems impossible. We submit our thoughts to God and trust more in his promises than in our own calculations. Let us dare to reach the impossible, "for nothing is impossible with God" (Luke 1:37; Matthew 19:26).

The shield of faith is our source of power in the spiritual battle against the powers of darkness (Ephesians 6:16). These powers act in the socioeconomic and political structures of our society. Faith frees us from the discouragement that comes from the continual attacks of the enemy. These may come in a variety of ways, including other persons and institutions. Failure can easily and quickly wound our faith. The enemy knows how to deceive our mind and feelings to paralyze our will. This weakens our faith. Therefore, it is necessary to strengthen our faith by prayer and praise. Abraham, the father of faith, was also beset by doubts, but he resisted them. He was "strengthened in his faith and gave glory to God" (Romans 4:20). For "this is the victory that has overcome the world, even our faith" (1 John 5:4).

Doubt, as such, is not the enemy of faith. The great enemy of faith is unbelief, desperation, being afraid of acting for fear of making a mistake. It is not wanting to suffer, or it is losing hope of triumph. But life in the world is overcome by faith. Therefore, the prayer that accompanies obedience will be a prayer of faith. We are to cast aside doubt (James 1:6) and every root of bitterness that leads us to unbelief and disobedience (Hebrews 3:18, 19).

The apostle John states a similar truth: "This is the assurance we have in approaching God: that if we ask anything according to his will, he hears us. And if we know that he hears us—whatever we ask—we know that we have what we asked of him" (1 John 5:14-15). Jesus knew by experience this principle of the prayer of faith. He urged his disciples, "whatever you ask for in prayer, believe that you have received it, and it will be yours" (Mark 11:24).

When we undertake the walk of faith, we put our trust in the power of God. Our obedience is the sincere proof of our faith in God. We seek to do the will of the Father rather than to satisfy our own thoughts. When we follow Jesus in doing the justice of God, we will experience moments of sadness and weeping. Not even God himself could avoid this pain. Through this innocent suffering we will share the sufferings of Christ. By the grace of God we also will be able to share his own divine nature. This obedience of faith places us fully in the depths of the heart of God. God wants and the world needs

Christians who struggle for justice out of obedience to their faith. For the just shall live by faith and thus will please God (Hebrews 10:38; Habakkuk 2:3, 4).

The Power of the Spirit

Jesus' life and teachings outline for us the way of justice in God's kingdom. However, if we try to live these teachings by our own strength, we soon discover our utter weakness. For example, if we attempt to fulfill the teachings of the Beatitudes (Matthew 5:3-10), we soon become burdened rather than liberated.

Righteousness is a fruit of the Holy Spirit and the outgrowth of a life in Christ. Paul affirms this truth: "You were taught, with regard to your former way of life, to put off your old self, which is being corrupted by its deceitful desires; to be made new in the attitude of your minds; and to put on the new self, created to be like God in true righteousness and holiness.... For the fruit of the light consists in all goodness, righteousness and truth" (Ephesians 4:22-24; 5:9).

The justice of the kingdom cannot be lived apart from the Spirit of God. This is why Jesus, before ascending to the Father, promises to send the disciples the Comforter, the Helper.

As pilgrims passing through a foreign land, we are not to live conformed to the tendencies of the present society. Instead, our goal is to live God's "good, pleasing and perfect will" (Romans 12:2b). Social justice is a way of life and such a lifestyle becomes an instrument of peace. But it has its limits. The justice of God involves all of life. It includes salvation from sin and the human tendency toward sin and evil. Our actions as Christians are not founded on currents of modern thought. Such thinking says one needs to be an activist and give long speeches on social justice. Frequently this activism hides great problems, even sin, hidden and justified by an outward justice and by words. Among peace-loving persons it is easy to find violent persons who talk and struggle for peace, but who do not have peace; who seek justice for the poor but are opposed to speaking of "sin," "repentance," and "salvation."

Our basis for peace and justice is the Bible. Its teachings lead us to live justice in all our life, in harmony with the wisdom of God. "But the wisdom that comes from heaven is first of all pure; then peace loving, considerate, submissive, full of mercy and good fruit, impartial and sincere. Peacemakers who sow in peace raise a harvest of righteousness" (James 3:17-18). "For the kingdom of God is . . . righteousness, peace and joy in the Holy Spirit" (Romans 14:17). Everyone who lives in the power of the Spirit will not use false claims and promises to establish justice. Rather, in all his life he will live a life that is true to the teachings and example of Jesus. In the same way, everyone who lives in the power of the Spirit will not be content with a life of personal piety and salvation. Instead, he will create situations of justice and will be willing to give his life for those who suffer.

This is what Jesus did when, full of the Holy Spirit, he exclaimed: "The Spirit of the Lord is on me, because he has anointed me to preach good news to the poor . . ." (Luke 4:18). This is the way we, his disciples, live. For the same Spirit that acted in him also acts in us.

Communities of Justice

How can we announce with power the justice of the kingdom if we ourselves do not live the will of God? How can we have authority and be heard by the world when we present the values of the kingdom of God? As we speak about God and share the divine promises we can say to the listener: "Come and see" (John 1:46). However, the strongest witness is to live the teachings of Jesus in daily life. This will show that in God a world of justice, peace, and love is possible. Our life will show how to create contexts of work, of recreation, of life that transmits the justice of God. We will live together with our brethren in the midst of problems and find solutions in the faith that unites us. This is community. This is church. This is what God wants of us while we are pilgrims in this world which is not our true home.

How everything has changed since the times of the early church. Being a Christian then meant death for confessing Jesus as Lord rather than Caesar! The history of the church is the history of the world. A world of interests and struggles for obtaining power. A world of injustices and wars, of corruption and hate, of evil and misery—of lives that do not know what it is to love God. But there are signs of change. Today one hears talk of returning to our roots, of renewing the church, of planting justice and pardon. People want to create communities of hope where they can live in a better world. God's way is a world of happiness and life, a world of reconciliation and true love. This is possible today through the power of God. By responding to God through Christ, there is a whole new world. In him, we are a new creation; in him, God has reconciled us to himself and has given us the ministry of reconciliation (2 Corinthians 5:17, 18).

If there is any hope for the world, it should be found among the people of God. This hope is found when Christians live as communities of justice, communities of forgiveness and of love. Christ did not intend to create a mass of religious people, believers, who do not live daily the evangelical message of justice and salvation! Rather, he wants cell groups where the peace of God is breathed deeply, where the surrender of lives is real, where serving and loving others springs from the heart. These communities of justice serve as oases in the middle of a desert, as points of light in the midst of darkness. Such communities show that salvation is in Jesus, that the Bible is very important, that power is found in God.

Let us help to create communities where the justice of God is lived in daily life; where there are no differences between rich and poor; where all the gifts are shared according to the needs. In such communities, the ones who govern are the ones who serve. Here authority is understood in the strategy of the cross. Here the world sees that God is real, that the good news of the gospel can be fulfilled. The injustices and disorders of society find an answer in this type of community life. Here the Word of God and the power of the Holy Spirit make the life of Jesus a reality. And from this community, we find strength to work toward justice for the poor and the oppressed. We become the voice of those without voice. We confront the authorities with their responsibility of doing justice. These efforts have a strong influence when they are supported by communities of justice that live what they require of others. These actions provide continuity to the message of the love and peace of Jesus.

Communities of Forgiveness

This challenge of doing justice does not consist in producing outstanding results. It consists in obedience, humility, and forgiveness. It is a willingness to give life to anyone who is seeking, whatever their situation: the lonely, the sick, the destitute, the rejected, and hopeless. Juan Cruz, a drug addict who came to our community is an example. He had attempted suicide twice. Psychiatrists were unable to understand him. He had been confined without hope of a cure. He came to us as a last resort, as a last chance for help. Slowly he found joy. He began to talk and finally to accept forgiveness. Now he is a walking miracle among us, following the Master, working with the team, discipling others, and experiencing salvation. The same is true for many others who were dead and now live by the grace of God.

An important aspect of these communities of justice is treating the offender with love and forgiveness. It is reconciling the divisions and living in humility and meekness, "for he himself is our peace" (Ephesians 2:14). "Be completely humble and gentle; be patient, bearing with one another in love. Make every effort to keep the unity of the Spirit through the bond of peace" (Ephesians 4:2, 3). As we give and receive correction from others who are in Christ, the justice of God becomes a reality. We carry each other's burdens and in this way fulfill the law of Christ, which is love (Galatians 6:1, 2).

Jesus gave his disciples the commandment of forgiveness. He gave his disciples authority to redeem or retain sins (John 20:23), to bind and loose (Matthew 18:18), to exercise discipline, to correct the one who sins. Those who refused to accept correction were put out of the fellowship. All of this is necessary to maintain justice in the community of forgiveness. We take this order from God seriously because we know that, although saved, we are still in the flesh; we're still subject to fall into temptation. Furthermore, judgment is "to begin with the family of God" (1 Peter 4:17). That is why we must judge those within the communities of justice. God has said he will judge those that are outside (1 Corinthians 5:12, 13). When we judge a brother, we seek his restoration, because God always pardons the one who repents. That love that covers a multitude of sins will persuade the brother in his error (Proverbs 10:12; James 5:19, 20).

The Injustice of Evil

On a trip to the United States I was horrified by what I saw in New York City. Similar things are happening in Paris, Buenos Aires, London, Amsterdam, etc. Passing through Manhattan in New York we came to the famous 42nd Street. Although we had been told about the atmosphere, the evil defied imagination. At late hours of the night we saw many boys and girls in the chaos of lights, drugs, alcohol, violence, and sexual perversion. Alone or in pairs, they wandered from one side of the street to the other. They entered and left centers of games and diversion. They were only nine or ten years old. We talked with some and learned that they lived on the street. They knew much more about that world of evil than of their own families. They were already professionals of prostitution.

They didn't care who they sold themselves to as long as they could find something to eat. The police would come and take them away. That night they would sleep in safety. However, the next day the struggle on the street would resume. Seeing that absurd, grotesque spectacle, that unjust crime that society was committing, tied my stomach in knots. I wanted to cry, scream, struggle. What could be done for those children? Where will this rotten society take us?

There are other evils: the threat of nuclear holocaust, the chasm between rich and poor, the injustice, oppression, and suppression of human rights, the violence of wars, tortures, and invasions. Hunger, corruption, and an abundance of tyrants weigh heavily on this small planet, so mistreated, so exploited. Contamination spreads like gangrene. Landscapes are destroyed. Animals are extinguished. Earthquakes, volcanoes, storms, pollution of the air, upset the laws of nature. Jails grow. Mental hospitals are increased. Drugs and alcohol drown their victims in a slow but fatal end. Collective suicide? The triumph of death? Where is the sense of history? What is God doing in light of so much pain? "We know that the whole creation has been groaning as in the pains of childbirth . . . as we wait . . . the redemption of our bodies" (Romans 8:22, 23).

6

THE FUTURE OF GOD WILL BRING JUSTICE

THE Apostle John, exiled on the Island of Patmos, faced an uncertain future. As he suffered for his faith, he also wondered what would happen to him. However, he didn't despair, but trusted God. Through faith he saw a new heaven and a new earth where "there will be no more death or mourning or crying or pain" (see Revelation 21:1-4). And John speaks of a day in which a rider, "Faithful and True" will come. He will not tarry but with justice will judge the nations. And his name is the Word of God. And out of his mouth comes a sharp sword with which to strike down the nations (Revelation 19:11-15). The slain Lamb is the only one able to open the book of life. He is worthy to receive power, riches, wisdom, strength, honor, glory, and praise (Revelation 5:6-12). And his enemies will come.

> They will make war against the Lamb, but the Lamb will overcome them because he is Lord of lords and King of kings—and with him will be his called, chosen and faithful followers. Revelation 17:14.
>
> Then I saw another angel flying in midair, and he had the eternal gospel to proclaim to those who live on the earth—to every nation, tribe, language and people. He said in a loud voice, "Fear God and give him glory, because the hour of his judgment has come. Worship him who made the heavens, the earth, the sea and the springs of water." Revelation 14:6, 7.
>
> Let him who does wrong continue to do wrong . . . let him who does right continue to do right. . . . Behold, I am coming soon! My reward is with me, and I will give to everyone according to what he has done. Revelation 22:11, 12.
>
> He who testifies to these things says, "Yes, I am coming soon." Amen. Come, Lord Jesus. Revelation 22:20.

Because this vision confirms all the messianic prophecies, we can wait for Jesus' final victory. This will occur on "the day of the Lord" that "will come like a thief" (2 Peter 3:10). This is our hope. The future is God's, and we who are in God should not fear the future. The world trembles before a future of decay and destruction. "But in keeping with his promise we are looking forward to a new heaven and a new earth, the home of righteousness" (2 Peter 3:13). How and when will all this happen? We do not know when or how. It is not for us to know. We can affirm that it will happen. Because Jesus reveals to us the meaning of life, the key of history, we can live with hope. The triumph of the cross will one day have its universal effect.

The Final Judgment

When the Son of Man comes in his glory, and all the angels with him, he will sit on his throne in heavenly glory. All the nations will be gathered before him, and he will separate the people one from another as a shepherd separates the sheep from the goats. He will put the sheep on his right and the goats on his left. Then the King will say to those on his right, "Come, you who are blessed by my Father; take your inheritance, the kingdom prepared for you since the creation of the world . . . ." Then he will say to those on his left, "Depart from me, you who are cursed, into the eternal fire prepared for the devil and his angels." Matthew 25:31-34, 41.

This judgment is not so far away. We can already begin to feel the imminent weight of that time in which God will fulfill his final justice. We, the Christians, "must be ready, because the Son of Man will come at an hour when you do not expect him" (Matthew 24:44). "Therefore put on the full armor of God, so that when the day of evil comes, you may be able to stand your ground, and after you have done everything, to stand. Stand firm then, with the belt of truth buckled around your waist, with the breastplate of righteousness in place" (Ephesians 6:13, 14). In the time that remains we must announce to an unbelieving world the truths of God. Furthermore, we must do it without fear and without resorting to unclear language—sweet ambiguities. Surely some will turn to God in repentance when they see our sincere lives and hear the prophetic words announcing the end.

James clearly denounces injustice and announces God's final justice:

Now listen, you rich people, weep and wail because of the misery that is coming upon you. Your wealth has rotted, and moths have eaten your clothes. Your gold and silver are corroded. Their corrosion will testify against you and eat your flesh like fire. You have hoarded wealth in the last days. Look! The wages you failed to pay the workmen who mowed your fields are crying out against you. The cries of the harvesters have reached the ears of the Lord Almighty. You have lived on earth in luxury and self-indulgence. You have fattened yourselves in the day of slaughter. You have condemned and murdered innocent men, who were not opposing you. James 5:1-6.

To those who have trusted in God's promises and waited for his justice, James says: "Be patient, then, brothers, until the Lord's coming. See how the farmer waits for the land to yield its valuable crop and how patient he is for the fall and spring rains. You too, be patient and stand firm, because the Lord's coming is near" (James 5:7, 8).

We who have put our lives in the cross don't have anything to fear. The victory of Jesus is already a reality. In our world, Jesus is already Lord. His power already reigns among us. We hope for the fullness of time when everything will be fulfilled. On that day he will establish his final justice under the supreme Judge. Meanwhile we do not faint. We struggle and keep the flame of the light of Christ alive in our lives. We fill the earth with the salt that makes it possible to live in the world.

We are called to share the victory of Christ. In the time that remains until the final day we are to work for righteousness and love. Paul prays for us that we "may be pure and blameless until the day of Christ, filled with the fruit of righteousness that comes through Jesus Christ—to the glory and praise of God" (Philippians 1:9-11). And in the "final judgment" when God reestablishes his order and justice,

many will awake to "shame and everlasting con-
tempt." However, "those who lead many to
righteousness [will shine] like the stars for ever and
ever" (Daniel 12:2, 3).

CONCLUSION

JESUS teaches us to "walk while you have the light" (John 12:35). If we walk in his light, darkness will not overtake us. Furthermore, his light will guide us along the way of biblical justice.

Since I am the youngest son of a Spanish Catholic family, my parents wanted me to be a priest. When I was eleven years old, I enrolled in a seminary of the Dominican Order. From early childhood until now I have always had a great sensitivity for justice. Seminary also helped me develop a critical attitude toward every form of oppression.

When I left the Catholic seminary, I migrated to Belgium to study languages while I worked. Belgium is one of the countries in Europe that gave the best welcome to immigrants in the 1960s. But even here immigrants faced great discrimination. For example, if one went to rent a house, one often found the sign *"etrangers s'abstenir"* (foreigners not admitted). The same thing occurred when looking for a job. One had to accept the hardest jobs, the ones the people of the country didn't want. One not only earned less for more work and paid the same taxes, one also was accused of having come to steal bread from the Belgians by taking away their jobs. In reality, the foreign work force was required to maintain the industrial development and high level of life in the country. As an immigrant, I not only felt indignation for the injustices I witnessed; I also suffered them. I felt defenseless before that discrimination.

I found one exception in my contacts as an immigrant which changed my whole life. The mission agency of the Mennonite Church had opened an office to help foreign workers. This social service not only got jobs for many Spaniards; it also led to the beginning of the Mennonite Church in Brussels. It was there that I had a personal encounter with Jesus as my Savior and Lord. Later on I became one of the leaders of this church, working with the Spanish immigrants. Presently many of us that were accepted by that social service are ministering in Spain. We are happy that we found not only work but, above all, salvation in Jesus and a Christian lifestyle.

It was not the intention of that social service to attract foreigners so they would come to church, although some did come because of it. The intention was to be faithful to Jesus and provide a solution, small as it was, to an important need at that moment. It was an attempt to remedy an injustice. How? It taught the foreigners their legal rights and helped them find a solution to their problems of work and adaptation. And the fruits of that justice was salvation for many. Here we see the close relationship between our commitment to justice and our announcement of the good news of salvation in Jesus.

The Anabaptists since the 16th century have emphasized a Christian life that expressed both word and deed. The Catholic Church then had come to understand good works as separate acts of a life of faith and as merits to gain salvation. Luther and his followers did not accept James' insistence that faith without works is a dead faith; that it was Abraham's faith coupled with his actions that credited him with righteousness and caused him to be called the friend of God (James 2:20-26). The Anabaptists took Luther's reform seriously, but they went even further. They were not content with only good doctrine or faith alone or the Scriptures alone; rather, they put their emphasis on the teachings of the Sermon on the Mount—radical discipleship and sharing material goods. There was no distinction between rich and poor in their assemblies. They all shared with simplicity and unity of heart. In obedience to Jesus, many persons formed communities of love. Some of these continue even today (Hutterites). The faith of these Anabaptists was so strong that they were willing to die for it. Their love and nonviolence led them to save even the lives of those who persecuted and martyred them.

It is also true that over the centuries many Mennonites have lost the Anabaptist vision. They have been fed spiritually by a Protestant tradition. It has moved them away from the authentic balance found by their ancestors, the Anabaptists. But more recently some have tried to recapture that Anabaptist vision in theory and practice. Communities have been formed to more faithfully live out the teachings of Jesus. The emphases of these groups have done much good for the body of Christ in general and the Mennonite churches in particular.

How good it would be if many Mennonites rediscovered the richness of the Anabaptist vision. Both traditional and progressive members could benefit from a renewed emphasis on the harmony between faith and lifestyle! A life of holiness and a life of righteousness have the same meaning in Anabaptist thinking as in the Bible. The Anabaptists saw a balance between spiritual and personal life and community commitment. This balance also included all the material and practical aspects of daily life. It was a radical discipleship. It means taking the lordship of Jesus—his rule in our lives—seriously. This costly way of the cross contrasts sharply with the distortions of the gospel that so many religious movements are making.

May the light (truth) that we have received from Jesus and from those who were faithful to his life and message radiate energy and power to a world of darkness! The injustices in the lives of so many people and in the structures of our society not only must be denounced, a new solution must be offered—the authentic power of Jesus and his cross.

This solution must first be lived by those who proclaim it. Only then will it be believable.

For if "the light within you is darkness, how great is that darkness!" (Matthew 6:23).

While we have light, we will walk in justice and lead others in that way. Jesus has called us the light of the world and the salt of the earth. Light cannot be hidden; it should shine before men so when they see our works of righteousness they will give glory to God. Salt slows the process of corruption and gives a good flavor. Our righteousness should be like light and salt amid a society of darkness and oppression. We can hope for the world to change only if we help to change the small part close to us.

> Justice will dwell in the desert and righteousness live in the fertile field. The fruit of righteousness will be peace; the effect of righteousness will be quietness and confidence forever.
>
> Isaiah 32:16, 17.

FOR FURTHER READING AND STUDY

Driver, John. *Community and Commitment*, Herald Press, Scottdale, Pa., 1976.

_____ *Kingdom Citizens*, Herald Press, Scottdale, Pa., 1980.

Escobar, Samuel, and John Driver. *Christian Mission and Social Justice*, Herald Press, Scottdale, Pa., 1978.

Hess, J. Daniel. *Integrity*, Herald Press, Scottdale, Pa., 1978.

Keeney, William. *Lordship as Servanthood*, Faith and Life Press, Newton, Kan., and Mennonite Publishing House, Scottdale, Pa., 1975.

Miller, John W. *The Christian Way*, Herald Press, Scottdale, Pa., 1969.

Nelson, Jack A. *Hunger for Justice: The Politics of Food and Faith*, Maryknoll, N.Y., 1980.

Sider, Ronald J. *Evangelism, Salvation and Social Justice*, Grove Books, Bramcote, Notts (England), 1975, 1977.

Wallis, Jim. *Agenda for Biblical People*, Harper & Row, New York, N.Y., 1976.

_____ *The Call to Conversion*, Harper & Row, New York, N.Y., 1981.

José Gallardo ministers in churches and intentional communities in Burgos, Spain, as well as in some other countries of Europe. He was born in Albacete, Spain, and raised Catholic. At the age of 11, he attended a Catholic seminary of the Dominican Order.

After completing high school, he went to Belgium as a migrant worker. Here he met the Mennonites through their relief and social service activities among Spanish migrants. After he became a member of the local church, he received a call to prepare for full-time Christian service.

From 1968 to 1970 he studied at the Mennonite Seminary in Montevideo, Uruguay, and during 1971-72 he attended Goshen Biblical Seminary in Elkhart, Indiana. Later he completed his theological studies in Brussels with a thesis on discipleship and nonviolence.

While in South America, he worked with inmates in

the prisons of Montevideo, served Mennonite churches in Uruguay and Argentina, and worked with Mennonite Central Committee workers in the region of Santa Cruz, Bolivia. Later he assisted migrant workers in Europe, taught New Testament and social ethics part-time at the Bienenberg Bible School in Liestal, Switzerland, and worked as a delegate of the International Red Cross.

In 1975 he was ordained as an itinerant preacher and teacher at a European Colloquium of the Mennonite Board of Missions in London and as a part-time pastor of the Spanish Mennonite Church in Brussels.

In 1978 he returned to Spain and joined a renewal movement among young people in Burgos. In the nearby village of Quintanadueñas he helped to start a community of rehabilitation for drug addicts, delinquents, and outcasts. From here he continues an itinerant ministry among churches and small fellowship groups in Spain and other countries of Europe.

MENNONITE FAITH SERIES

Edited by
Elizabeth Showalter and J. Allen Brubaker

This series of books sets forth briefly and simply some of the major emphases of the New Testament as understood in the Anabaptist-Mennonite tradition—a faith which represents a cluster of emphases somewhat in contrast with those of the major bodies of Christendom in the sixteenth century: Roman Catholic, Orthodox, Anglican, Lutheran, and Reformed.

1. *How Mennonites Came to Be* by J. C. Wenger
2. *What Mennonites Believe* by J. C. Wenger
3. *The Way to a New Life* by J. C. Wenger
4. *The Way of Peace* by J. C. Wenger
5. *Disciples of Jesus* by J. C. Wenger
6. *The Way of True Riches* by Milo Kauffman
7. *Teaching in the Congregation*
   by Paul M. Lederach
8. *The Book We Call the Bible* by J. C. Wenger
9. *A Faith to Live By* by J. C. Wenger
10. *The Family of Faith* by J. C. Wenger
11. *The Way of Biblical Justice* by José Gallardo
12. *Evangelism as Discipling* by Myron S. Augsburger

The books in this series are published in North America by:

HERALD PRESS
616 Walnut Avenue
Scottdale, Pa. 15683

HERALD PRESS
117 King Street, West
Kitchener, Ont. N2G 4M5

Overseas persons wanting copies of the booklets or permission to translate should write to: Mennonite Board of Missions, 1251 Edom Road, Harrisonburg, Va. 22801.